This is a wonderful book! Rick Gertsema draws upon his years of interactions with families to create a developmentally based strategy for parents. His thoughtful examples and practical suggestions are extraordinarily valuable.

—Gordon Harvieux, M.D., F.A.A.P., Medical Director, Duluth Children's Medical Home Program

Rick Gertsema understands kids. He is realistic, insightful, and down to earth. Kids appreciate his frankness, honesty, and understanding. He is passionate about helping children understand themselves and how they function in the world. He is relentless but kind in exploring the emotional pain driving their behaviors. He works effectively with parents, helping them understand their child, effective parenting and the journey to recovery. But most of all he helps children and their families heal.

—Patricia Burns
President, Miller D___ ___ ___ ___on

peaceful & practical
parenting

Andrea,
Blessings in
your future!
Rick

peaceful & practical
parenting
RICK GERTSEMA

Tate Publishing & Enterprises

Published by Tate Publishing & Enterprises, LLC
127 E. Trade Center Terrace | Mustang, Oklahoma 73064 USA
1.888.361.9473 | www.tatepublishing.com

Tate Publishing is committed to excellence in the publishing industry. The company reflects the philosophy established by the founders, based on Psalm 68:11,
"The Lord gave the word and great was the company of those who published it."

Book design copyright © 2010 by Tate Publishing, LLC. All rights reserved.
Cover design by Kellie Southerland
Interior design by Blake Brasor

Published in the United States of America

ISBN: 978-1-61663-664-7
1. Family & Relationships, Parenting, General
2. Family & Relationships, Life Stages, General
10.06.21

dedication

To Carrie, my partner in life and parenting

table of
contents

introduction

As a master's-level, licensed psychologist, I have had the opportunity to work in a number of different settings, including residential treatment, home-based services, and outpatient mental health settings. My career in behavioral health started in 1982 when I was working in an adult psychiatric setting.

I am currently working with children and adolescents in a family practice outpatient setting, and I am often asked, "Is there a book some place that I can read that talks about the ideas that you share with us in therapy?"

This book is my attempt to put into writing many of the tools that I have learned and used in my own clinical practice. Many of the ideas are modified and borrowed from others who have worked successfully with children. However, the bulk of the ideas come via the most important people of all—the parents, children, and adolescents with whom I have had the opportunity to work. In addition, I have had the blessing and opportunity to be married for over twenty-five years and have two beautiful daughters who have taught me more than I ever thought I could know. Now, for reminder purposes, as I am writing this book, I have a granddaughter who is willing to teach me all over again!

Rick Gertsema

It is my sincere hope that the contents of this book will be helpful to you, your family, and your children.

developmental
milestones

A Child is not a vessel to be filled but a lamp to be lit.

—Unknown

Children are likely to live up to what you believe of them.

—Lady Bird Johnson

In order to fully understand our children and what to expect from them, it is important for us to have a framework from which we can operate. Therefore, for the purposes of this book, developmental milestones will be outlined for infancy (0–18 months), toddler (1–3 years), preschool (4–6 years), school-age (7–12 years), and adolescence (13–19 years). These developmental stages are offered as a range and not an absolute of what to expect for every child in each stage of development. Individual differences are to be expected, not seen as abnormal.

These stages are important because they are the foundation for all of our interactions with youth. If we think about building a home, we need to make sure there is a strong, well-built foundation to support the house for decades. This is the purpose of the developmental milestones for our children.

In addition, the milestones offer us a road map to help gauge what could be considered normal for our children. As parents, we are constantly asking ourselves or others, "Do you think this is normal behavior?" The developmental milestones give us a range of normal for each of the age groups through age nineteen.

Rick Gertsema

The following pages will outline the specific developmental milestones in each age group or stage. Also outlined are play patterns, developmental tasks, and central values and themes. In addition, there is a section on appropriate environmental inputs (parenting).

Interspersed between the outlines for each stage are narratives and descriptions of what to expect in each stage. Much of the language used in the outlines may sound clinical or academic. It is important to be able to put the stages into a day-to-day, practical framework.

The categories of the outline pages are:

- Developmental Milestones: what we can expect to see, measure, or witness with our children. Developmental milestones are observable for each stage of development.
- Play Patterns: the language of children. How children play can show us much about the child and their stage of development. The patterns can represent social skills, interpersonal skills, and self-modulation of emotion.

- Developmental Tasks: what is happening internally within children as they grow.
- Central Values and Themes: like a summary at the end of a chapter in a book. Each stage of development has a specific theme. All of the themes combined create the book that must be completed by a child in order to move into healthy adulthood.
- Appropriate Environmental Inputs: a way of asking, "How do we parent during this developmental stage?"

The purpose of sharing the developmental milestones from ages zero through nineteen is to remind us that the categories apply to all stages of development, not just infancy and the elementary school years. As the milestones are reviewed on the following pages, we see good reasons for our children acting the way they do—it is called development.

It is important to remember that children must go through all of the developmental milestones and the developmental tasks in order to achieve healthy adulthood. Each stage builds on the successful completion of the previous one. If there has been some trauma or crisis in a child's life during a specific period, they

Rick Gertsema

may get stuck in a specific developmental milestone or task. We also see that children may regress to a previous stage of development when a new child is brought into the family, whether through birth or adoption. When children get stuck, our primary goal is to help them complete the developmental milestone or task, so they can, in a sense, catch up with themselves. With the regressed child, we can expect a return to their acquired developmental level once they have adjusted to the major change in their life.

Infancy (0-18 months)

Developmental Milestones:

- 3 months—social smile
- 6 months—differential response to a specific person
- 8 months—stranger and separation anxiety, sit alone, crawl
- 12 months—walk, begin to speak

Play Patterns:

- Solitary play
- Sensory motor exploration play

Developmental Tasks:

- Establish social bonds
- Attachment, sense of basic trust and security

Central Values and Themes:

- Hope
- To "get"
- To "take"

Appropriate Environmental Inputs:

- Trustworthy, nurturing parenting
- Physical contact
- Comfort
- Adequate nutrition
- Relationship promotion
- Stimulating interaction with warm, loving, and responsive adult(s)
- Patient nurturing—caring, warm, giving, comforting, unconditional love

As children grow, the basic architecture of the brain is constructed through an ongoing process that begins

Rick Gertsema

before birth and continues into adulthood. The early years of life are critical, because early experiences affect the architecture of the maturing brain. The early years form either a sturdy or a fragile foundation for all of the development and behavior that follows. Experts are learning more and more about how interactions with other people affect the development of babies' brains. As it turns out, the healthy development of brain architecture depends a lot on a kind of interaction experts call "serve and return," which is based on an analogy from games like tennis and volleyball.

"Serve and return" happens when young children instinctively reach out for interaction through babbling, facial expressions, words, gestures, cries, etc., and adults respond by doing the same kind of babbling, gesturing, and so forth. Young children need many of these interactions per day, since they are so critical to development and have effects on everything from the chemicals in the brain to physical structure and brain cell connections. These loving actions are often described as building attachment and are a key protective factor in the developing brain of infants and young children. The positive effects literally last a lifetime. The more we, as parents, can educate ourselves on the internal needs of our children, the better the outcomes for the entire family.

Infancy is likely the most concrete and self-explanatory stage of development, yet there are some points that warrant discussion and clarification. First, in developmental milestones, by the time an infant is about six months old, he or she is making social smiles and having different responses to different people—a differential response. At about eight months old, infants start to have stranger anxiety and separation anxiety. When they are handed to an adult they don't know well, they will start to cry. This is the time when babies start wailing when Mom and Dad leave them with the babysitter. It can be challenging for parents to go out during this stage.

In terms of play patterns, the most notable activity infants are involved in is discovering their bodies. For example, babies can lie on the bed and be amazed and occupied looking at their fingers or feet for long periods of time.

The primary developmental task for this stage of development is attachment, or a sense of basic and absolute trust and security with parents or caregivers. Infants can be held away with outstretched arms by a parent, bounced on the knee, and sometimes tossed in the air, and they will simply smile or laugh. This is a reflection of their absolute trust in their parents.

Infancy is a stage of development that holds great

hope. Other themes and values are the infants learning how to "get" from others, and also how to "take."

This is the stage of giving a child unconditional love—cuddling, patient nurturing, and stimulating interactions with warm, loving, and responsive adults. These are appropriate environmental inputs (parenting). Attunement with the infant is the parental goal—learning to understand the language of the baby and being with them where they are. During this stage of development, parents can pay very close attention to the sounds and noises their baby is making. Depending on the baby's needs, there can be very different sounds and cries. One cry may be the baby wanting to eat; another may be a reflection of the baby being uncomfortable. The tendency is to simply go to the baby immediately if they are making crying noises. Before picking them up, however, listen to the noises, and then start to pair the cries with the need that is discovered. Babies have a language all their own very early in life.

> Babies have a language all their own very early in life.

It is also important during this stage to allow the baby the time to develop sounds and language by allowing them to coo and make comfortable sounds. There is certainly no harm in letting a baby lie in the crib and make content noises. Listen to that language as well.

Toddlers (1-3 years)

Developmental Milestones:

- Speech
- Toilet training
- Limits and self-control
- Self-assertion
- Physical independence

Play Patterns:

- Parallel play with peers
- Mastery, skill-oriented play

Developmental Tasks:

- Separation/individuation
- Sense of autonomy, self-assertion
- Object constancy, stability in relationships
- Self-control of aggression and impulse

Rick Gertsema

Central Values and Themes:

- Separateness from parents
- Discovery
- Exploration
- Autonomy

Appropriate Environmental Inputs:

- Judicious parental persons
- Establishing separateness
- Consistent setting of limits and structure of environment
- Teaching impulse control and encouraging self-control
- Respect for autonomy and tolerance of self-assertion

In looking at the developmental milestones for one to three years, we see that children begin to speak and put together words that will give them the ability to communicate with others more effectively. Toilet training is typically completed during this stage of development. It is important to remember that toilet training cannot take place until a child has language to express his or her needs. This certainly doesn't mean that the child will be able to say the word "toilet," but he or she may point to it and want to try to sit on it. There is usually a natural curiosity that takes place when children see their mom, dad, or siblings go into the bathroom. If there is an interest, that can be the language to express their needs.

Children will also learn to assert themselves through the use of language and behavior. They will learn how to become physically independent from us, as demonstrated by being able to tolerate being in another room with no major distress. A typical behavior seen in this stage of development is when a child will go into another room, peek around the corner, and smile brightly or laugh when an adult acknowledges them. They are learning that even though they don't see us, they can rely on us still being in the other room. This is called object constancy and will be discussed further in the next section.

In play patterns, we see parallel play—where two children can sit together in the same area, be playing the same thing or doing the same thing, and they are content. We would also expect that children this age are developing a sense of mastery in what they are playing. Further, they are demonstrating skill-oriented play; they are using their bodies and their intellectual abilities to play. They are literally developing

Rick Gertsema

skills. It is here where the child may begin to be interested in rolling a ball back and forth—a predecessor to throwing the ball, which is an excellent relationship-building or enhancing activity. Games that combine words and action such as patty-cake, "This Little Piggy," or asking, "How big is the baby? So big!" with hands raised in the air—these are also fun at this age and develop language and interaction skills.

The developmental tasks for ages one to three include separation—individuation, which means that children have gained the sense that they are indeed a separate person from their mom, dad, or their primary caregiver. Internally, they are also gaining a sense of autonomy and self-assertion. This is often what is referred to as the "terrible twos," the age when children begin to have tantrums. What they are really doing is trying to demonstrate a sense of autonomy and self-assertion. One of the most direct and effective means for a child to assert himself or herself is to have a tantrum—to communicate his desires or dislikes. However, another developmental task during the toddler stage is for the toddler to display self-control of aggression and impulse. This is where the challenge of parenting enters. Here we need to understand that the temper tantrums are a healthy and normal part of development. As children develop their sense of self-control of aggression and impulse, there is a major decrease in tantrum behaviors. Children learn through active parenting that hitting, kicking, biting, and other aggressive behaviors are not acceptable. Parents are often saying "No!" and redirecting during this stage of development. If the fifteen-month-old is playing with the buttons on the stereo, a firm no, accompanied by moving him away and guiding his hands into a game of patty-cake, effectively changes the subject—for a while, at least.

Finally, by the end of this developmental stage, children have developed object constancy (knowing that parents can leave the room and still exist) and stability in relationships. They learn that Mom and Dad will be there when they wake in the morning—stability in the person or people who provide care for them and stability with grandparents and other significant people in their lives. Patterned, repetitive patterns of care throughout infancy and toddlerhood literally build pathways in the brain that guide our interactions throughout life.

In the appropriate environmental inputs area, this is a very active stage. The first challenge is the need to be judicious. Another way of saying this is to be as fair and consistent as possible in our parenting style from day to day and behavior to behavior. Toddlers are not

Rick Gertsema

concerned about whether or not Mom and Dad had a good day or bad day; they want things to be fair and predictable.

In this stage of development, parents need to establish separateness from their toddler. Games like peekaboo are an example of creating separateness. Creating this sense of separateness and reunion will instill a sense of trust and confidence in the toddler.

Consistent limits and structure of the environment are essential at this stage of development. Toddlers and older children look for—and like—predictability and structure. It is important to have consistent morning and bedtime routines at this time. This is also the stage where we are unsure about whether our child needs to nap. It is helpful for the toddler to know there is still quiet time in the middle of the day. If the toddler is tired, she will sleep. If not, she can spend quiet time in her room. Again, we are setting the stage for building a good sense of self and trust of the outside environment.

Finally, we need to teach impulse control and encourage self-control. We must demonstrate respect for autonomy and a tolerance of self-assertion. For example, as a toddler goes away from you into another room, when you have asked him to come to you, he is trying to show self-assertion. He also wants to be autonomous—to be the boss. Rather than getting upset with the toddler, respect that this is a developmental issue, and then bring him to where he needs to be so that he is in compliance with your parental request. It is not a power struggle of the terrible twos—just part of healthy development. This is quite a trick in parenting. The bottom line is that we need to demonstrate patience while our toddler may show us absolutely none. As long as we keep in mind that this is a necessary stage of development, it will likely be easier to exercise patience and persistence in parenting.

Preschool (4 - 6 years)

Developmental Milestones:

- Acquire social and sex roles
- Sibling rivalry
- Enculturation
- Social values and beliefs
- Conscience formation

Play Patterns:

- Cooperative play with peers
- Socio-dramatic play
- Rough-and-tumble play

Rick Gertsema

Developmental Tasks:

- Initiative
- Socialization
- Role learning
- Enculturation

Central Values and Themes:

- Purpose/direction
- Exploration
- Discovery
- Origination
- To "make" (go after)
- To "make like" (play/pretend)

Appropriate Environmental Inputs:

- Family models for social roles, customs, and behaviors
- Exposure to various social roles and cultural values
- Appropriate sex role modeling
- Peer interactions, social skill practice
- Identification with models

The developmental milestone for the preschool years is the stage where children start to take note of boys and girls acting differently. What it is to act like a boy or girl is in accordance to roles that they learn at home and at school. This process is also referred to as enculturation in the outline for this developmental stage. Directly related to acquiring social and sex roles is acquiring social values and social beliefs. These values and beliefs originate from the primary environments of the child—usually home and school.

During the preschool years, sibling rivalry starts to show itself. Siblings will start to show jealousy of one another and competition for attention from their parents and other caregivers. The beginning of forming a conscience occurs during this stage. This is the reason our children will cry, give us a dirty look, scowl, or look sad when we discipline them. They are starting to understand that they have done something wrong, and they feel badly about it or fear the consequences for their actions.

In terms of play patterns, this is the stage where we expect to see our children engaging in cooperative play with their peers. We will want and expect them to learn to share with their friends. As a matter of fact, this is one of the phrases that parents use in this stage of development—"We need to share our toys."

Rick Gertsema

In the outline, there is a reference to socio-dramatic play. This is another way of saying that our children will learn to take on certain roles in their play with one another. They may want to play dress up and take on the role of the mommy, the teacher, or the grandpa, for example. This is also the stage during which rough-and-tumble play begins for both boys and girls. Children may want to wrestle or play tackle football, for instance. Chasing and running is popular, accompanied by, "I'm going to beat you!"

The developmental task for preschool children during this stage is learning to take initiative. They may tell us that they would like to play a game or ask if they can help. They also begin the task of socializing with others, adults and children. As previously described, this is accomplished through enculturation and role learning.

The central themes and values for preschool children are to gain and display purpose and direction in what they are able to say and show us through their behavior. We want them to start showing a sense of determination. It is healthy and necessary for them to explore, discover, and demonstrate starting points of learning—to originate. We also want to see our children go after things that they seek, want, or are curious about, as well as copy or "make like" others through their play.

With regard to appropriate environmental inputs, this is the stage where children start to notice family models for social roles, customs, and behaviors. For example, the family custom that goes along with losing a tooth—like a visit from the tooth fairy, or for time spent with the family on holidays. In parenting our children at this stage, we talk out loud about what our practices and customs are so that our children can understand and practice those customs. We teach them why we do what we do as a family. These customs are not just for holidays or major events; they are also the day-to-day routines we practice as families. It is one of the true opportunities to start talking about the core family rules of love, respect, and honesty. Not only do we teach these by the words that we use in our interactions with our preschool children; we model them on a daily basis.

This is the stage where we start to expose our children to other social roles and cultural values. Children understand that other children and other families do things differently. They need assurance that this is not a matter of right or wrong; it is simply a different custom or value. It is fun at this stage to take children to plays, bookstores, libraries, and other places where

Rick Gertsema

they can experience the diversity of life. This is one of the reasons we want our children to spend time with peers—to experience and practice the social skills they have learned and had modeled for them.

We also want to model for our children what we believe are appropriate sex roles based on our own beliefs and values. What is typical male and female identity in our value system? How does the media view and present women and men and relationships between them? How are we in relationship to each other? A family discussion of "parts versus people" could be initiated at this stage.

During preschool years, children are also learning to identify with role models. They may start to make statements like, "I want to be a fireman," "I want to be a doctor," or "I want to be a teacher." This gives us the opportunity, as parents, to teach about each of these roles based on our own values.

School-age (7 - 12 years)

Developmental Milestones:

- Gang formation
- Peer and group identification
- Intellectual pursuit and growth of skills

Play Patterns:

- Organized, competitive and intellectual games
- Rough-and-tumble play
- Selective friendships

Developmental Tasks:

- Self-esteem based in productive activity
- Sense of productivity
- Sense of competency
- Group identity

Central Values and Themes:

- Skills
- Invention
- Construction
- Achievement, mastery
- To turn to
- To know how

Rick Gertsema

Appropriate Environmental Inputs:

- Instructive, supportive, facilitating adults
- Experiences of success and production
- Incentive for achievement
- Intellectual stimulation and school education
- Peer interactions
- Participation in peer group activities

As we review the developmental milestones for school-age children, it is quite clear that this stage is about children gaining a sense of belonging to a group and being involved in a learning system. At about age seven, we see our children starting to hang out with a group of kids. It is important to them to invite a number of other children to their birthday party, and it is also very important to tell others that they were invited to someone else's party. Children are trying to establish an association with a group separate from their primary family. This is why it is so difficult for children who are not invited to the parties; they want to belong.

For the children who are not invited, it is a great opportunity to talk about how it felt to not be invited. It will give children the chance to talk about their emotions openly and get validation for the way they feel. This will not only improve the parental relationship, but it will give the opportunity to do some problem solving together. One of the positive benefits could be the chance to have a party or get together with friends for more creative reasons other than a birthday party. It could be a popular theme, going to a movie, or doing a recreational activity together such as bowling. Just because your child was not invited to "that party" does not mean the other child would not be invited to this party. As a parent, keep in mind, there are always reasons for children to get together and celebrate being a child.

The other developmental milestone in this stage is for children to experience having their intellect challenged. Children are like a sponge for information at this stage of development. Obviously, children are in school of some type all day and are being challenged. However, it is also important that we continue to challenge our children in the home environment. Intellectually stimulating games are good for this age group. Even simple card games that challenge math skills can be helpful here. As parents, we will want to continue to assist our children in building on the skills developed in the earlier developmental stages.

Rick Gertsema

In regard to play patterns, this is the stage of development where we see children showing some need and desire for organization in their play with one another. They start to talk about the rules, and they like to have some sense of order to what they are playing. This is the stage where we begin to see competitive play—not just playing for fun but playing to win. Rough-and-tumble play continues, as was observed in the preschool stage. Another change during this stage is that selective friendships start to develop. Our children like to have their friends on their team or on their side. They will also start to exclude based on these friendships.

As we look at the developmental tasks for school-age children, we begin to observe that self-esteem is being built within our children based in productive activity. In other words, our children start to feel proud of the grades that they get or the results of their hard work. They need and appreciate parents and adults coming to see what they are able to accomplish. Children like to be helpers to adults at this stage of development because it helps them to feel good; they are being productive and competent. Older siblings like to hear that they are being a good big brother or big sister. As described in the developmental milestones, this is also the stage where children really begin to form group identity. This builds directly into the teenage years, when our adolescent's whole world is about relationships and their social life.

In reference to central values and themes, school-age children want to gain skills that they can use on a daily basis. They want to achieve, invent, and construct. When children in this age group master a task, there is a tremendous sense of accomplishment and pride. It is through these kinds of experiences that our children learn to know how—the sense of pride and mastery that they can accomplish tasks through their own skill and know-how. This is quite evident in schoolwork—for example, when a child is struggling with understanding a math task and feels like he just can't complete the task. As he successfully wrestles with the new concept and the light bulb comes on, he feels tremendous pride and accomplishment. Another example is when children are playing together and trying to build something or copy something that was built. Once they have succeeded in creating something, they want to show all the adults what they have accomplished.

The other theme is learning to *turn to*. In other words, children need to learn how and when to ask for help. As parents, we need to keep a watchful eye out for our opportunity to provide help, since asking for

Rick Gertsema

help is a difficult thing for younger school-age children. Using the same examples as above, when a child is struggling with a math concept, we want to help him or her. However, the child needs to come to the conclusion that he may need help. It is at this point that a parent can ask, "Do you need any help with your homework?" It is an opportunity for parents to extend help—teach them how to turn to and accomplish. Notice the wording of the question, however. It is, "Do you need help with your homework?" and not, "Don't you understand the math?"

During this stage of development, it is important to listen to what is *not* being said. Many times, children in this developmental stage are not able to articulate the needed words. They simply start getting "cranky." This is the opportunity to teach them to *turn to* by telling children, "I can see you are having a hard time. Is there anything I might be able to do to help?" We need to do this with confidence and support, as children are already in a position of feeling insecure about their world.

The other opportunity is to teach children to take a break from the stressful task and enjoy the experience of relationships with parents and family—to *turn to* for support. In such a task-oriented world, we tend to get locked into task completion rather than focus on the importance of relationships. We need to teach our children to face challenges with us, not alone. Try to keep in mind that during childhood and adolescence, behavior will speak louder than words.

With regard to appropriate environmental inputs (parenting), children in this stage of development need to have adults who are willing to teach and be supportive and patient while their child is in the process of learning. There is a tendency for parents to want to do things *for* their children at this age because it may be done more quickly. However, if we are doing things for our children all the time, they may never gain the experience of being productive and successful. When they have a difficult time, they can move through the difficulty to success and learn even more about themselves. They now can handle some adversity.

Parents and other adults need to provide incentive for achievement at this stage of development. This does not mean there needs to be material reward for every accomplishment. It does mean that children need praise and positive words specific to the accomplishment—not just "good job"—regardless of the size of the achievement.

 Rick Gertsema

> Children need praise and positive words specific to the accomplishment—not just "good job."

As described in previous sections, children at this age need to have intellectual stimulation and school education. This is what was described as children being sponges for new information. I truly believe children love to learn and will challenge themselves to learn when not discouraged by negative feedback from adults. Negative feedback from adults at this stage is usually interpreted by the child as rejection and disapproval. If a child feels rejection or disapproval, she may pair learning with this negative emotion and lose her innate curiosity and love for learning.

Finally, as children move through this stage of development, parents will notice more and more that their child seeks out peer interactions. Children want to be involved in peer group activities. Our challenge as parents is to help find the peer group activities that are a good fit for our child. It is not necessary to find a sport or activity to carry to excess; we are looking for opportunities for our children to learn how to successfully participate with peers. We do not need to be looking into the distant future and trying to get our child to become a professional athlete or qualify for college scholarships. Children practice social skills through interaction with friends in social settings or with teammates. Here are opportunities to address and resolve conflicts, express their emotions, and work through things. This, once again, is simply a necessary stage of development.

Adolescence (13 - 19)

Developmental Milestones:

- Body changes, rapid growth
- Cognitive development, abstract thought
- Sexual interest, relationships, and identity

Play Patterns:

- Social

Developmental Tasks:

- Sense of identity
- Sex role
- Independence from family
- Integration of personality
- Orientation of peer support

Rick Gertsema

Central Values and Themes:

- Devotion, fidelity
- Justice, sense of fairness
- Revolution
- Reformation
- Need to feel good
- To be oneself

Appropriate Environmental Inputs:

- Confirming parental adults, alternative mentors, and affirmative peers
- Consistent expectations with flexibility
- Tolerance and acceptance of the struggle
- Willingness to let go
- Respect and encouragement of individuation and autonomy

Welcome to the teenage years! This is an amazing stage of development that is all about change. In terms of the developmental milestones, we observe all of the obvious body changes that begin to happen. Our child is starting to look and sound more like a young adult by the time they are at the end of this stage. There are periods of rapid growth for many children, and teenagers constantly hear how much they have grown or how much they have changed. They are acutely aware of this and often self-conscious and confused about the many changes that are taking place.

Along with all of these external body changes, the brain is also changing as teenagers gain abstract thinking skills. This is the stage where adolescents will commonly state that they are not sure why they need to go to church; they don't know if they believe in a god. They may rethink or reprocess major changes that have happened in their lives, such as a divorce or other losses.

This is also the stage where our children become more sexual beings; they start to develop sexual interests, and we often say that their hormones are out of control. Again, as in the school-age stage of development, relationships are tremendously important. Adolescents are searching for and building their very own identity, again employing the context of their peer relationships for practice on a number of levels.

In reference to play patterns, it is nicely summed up in one word—social. Adolescents are social human beings. They like to do things together. It is common to hear teenagers say things like, "I need a social life, you know!" In this age of technology, there is instant messaging, text messaging, MySpace, Facebook, and

Rick Gertsema

cell phones. These are only vehicles for interaction, however. Nothing takes the place of face-to-face, hands-on, personal interactions. In middle school youth, for example, you may see groups of kids trying to squeeze through the doorway together in the school classroom. It appears that they are goofing around, but they are really just craving physical contact and a sense of connection.

The developmental task for adolescents is to gain a sense of identity. Who are they, and what do they want to think about doing with their lives? They begin to struggle with their own values and morals, especially in terms of the peers with whom they associate. They also begin to make decisions about sex roles and how each gender should act. This process started all the way back in the preschool years; now they will begin to solidify these ideas and concepts.

Adolescents want to start developing a sense of who they are separate from their family. They seek a sense of independence. In addition, they are trying to integrate all the parts of their personality that they have been building since the early stages of development. This will help them to become more oriented to their peer supports rather than just having family supports. It is very important at this stage for parents to remain open to conversation, state their own values, and acknowledge and allow the expression of teens' values and opinions, all the while keeping the core family values and clear expectations for safety at the forefront of family life.

As we read all of the developmental tasks that will be completed in this stage, it is obvious why we, as parents, become exhausted. As we watch our adolescents, we should be able to gain some insight into why they appear so chaotic to us. They are trying to complete many internal tasks while keeping up the adolescent pace of their external world. It is so very important to always try to keep in mind how this must feel to our teenagers.

In the words of the old song, "Try to remember and if you remember, then follow." Sometimes we need to just follow, especially in this stage of development. Follow our hearts, follow our intuition, and follow our love for our children!

> Try to remember how it felt when you were that age.

It is extremely important as parents, however, that we not attempt to redo our adolescence through our teens, whether via sports, school achievements, or social activities. This stage of development may be a trigger for adults, recalling the tumultuous years of their own adolescence. It is up to us to remain the adult now in support of our teens' best development. If we get caught in that old trap of, "I don't want you to make the same mistakes I did," we are not really listening to our teenager. Our teenager will feel like we are talking about ourselves and our past, and our past was a long time ago to them! This could be parenting out of our own fears or unresolved issues. We can remember what it was like to be a teenager, but we do not need to share those experiences unless we are invited by the teenager. Remembering does not mean talking about ourselves. Teenagers need us to listen, be present, confident, and patient enough to let them tell their whole story. Many times when teens have shared their stressful story, they will walk away feeling great, and the parent will be left feeling incomplete, worried, or like things are unresolved. This is part of parenting a teenager.

Adolescents are now developing a sense of devotion to self and others as central themes and values. Since they are also gaining a sense of sexual identity, they will start to gain a stronger sense of fidelity in relationships. Looking through the written comments in yearbooks or photo albums, a frequently-used statement is, "Thanks for always being there for me."

This is the stage of development where we commonly hear, "That's not fair." Adolescents are trying to acquire a sense of justice. As parents, we inform them, "Nobody ever said that life is fair." Adolescents commonly rebel against authority. They believe there needs to be reformation—a better way to interact with the world via different rules and guidelines. Teenagers have a need to feel good, and they are seeking their right to be themselves. This is seen in the way adolescents dress, the activities in which they participate, and the music they enjoy listening to on a regular basis.

In regard to appropriate environmental inputs, adolescents need to have affirming parental adults as well as other adults who can become healthy role models or mentors outside the family. They also seek peer relationships in which they gain affirmation. The need for positive reinforcement, praise, and attention may seem to be past, but in fact, it is not. A deficit in positive social interactions, whether within the home, at school, with peers, or in the greater community, puts teens at risk for use of alcohol and drugs or premature sexual activity. Although teens may appear to be young adults, they still need our guidance and attention, delivered in a positive and affirming manner, as we do our best to manage our fears and judgments during this phase of their developmental process.

Adolescents need consistent expectations with some flexibility. This will be discussed in greater

Rick Gertsema

detail later in this book in reference to the importance of parenting with love, respect, and honesty.

One of the greatest parenting challenges is to have tolerance and acceptance of the struggles of adolescence. This is one of the reasons that parenting a teenager can feel so exhausting. The other big reason is that, as parents, we need to begin letting go of our adolescents yet have some sense of confidence that they will come to us in times of need. It is something of a repeat of the exploration and activity we saw in the toddler stage.

The opportunity and the challenge for parents of adolescents are to give teenagers respect and encouragement for their struggle for individuation and autonomy. After all, we raised them to be independent young adults, so when they act that way, we need to respect that they are doing exactly what we hoped they would do. The typical kinds of statements from teenagers are, "You know I'm not a kid anymore. I am sixteen (or seventeen or eighteen) years old." This is the beginning of them trying to assert themselves as young adults or individuals. Rather than getting upset and trying to make sure the teenager understands that he or she is still a child who is living under "your roof," listen to what is being said under the statement: "I am trying my best to be the young adult that you want me to be, but I am not exactly sure how; help me!" As discussed, this is the chance for a parent to ask, "What can I do to help" or, "How can I help you figure this out?" Teenagers need to know there are still expectations for respect in relationships but there are solutions within those expectations.

One of the most important things to keep in mind is that adolescence is a time of great growth and change, not just for our teens but for our relationships with our children. Never succumb to the myth that teens do not need or want their parents to be involved with them. Be flexible, remain loving, listen, and continue to gently guide. This is the culmination of our hard word through all the stages. Don't miss out on it—enjoy it!

stages of
parenting

We worry about what a child will become tomorrow, yet we forget he is someone today.
—Stacia Tauscher

Making the decision to parent a child–it's momentous. It is to decide forever to have your heart go walking outside your body.
—Elizabeth Stone

As we think about parenting, I believe it is helpful to talk about three very distinct stages. The first stage is hands-on parenting. This stage is used in the stages of infancy, toddler, and preschool. These are the years where we find ourselves needing to check to see what our children are doing, physically redirect our children, and worry about them being too quiet. This is a physically busy stage of parenting.

The second stage of parenting is parent as a guide and director. In this stage of parenting, there is some still hands-on parenting, but we move toward more guidance and direction. This is the developmental stage of school-age, where children begin to move toward group and peer identification. In other words, they start needing Mom and Dad less than they did in previous stages. As parents, this is the stage where we encourage our children to play in the other room or go play outside with friends. We carefully observe from a distance and become a guide or director as needed. Our goal is to help our children learn how to socialize and reciprocate in relationships, as outlined in the previous chapter—"to turn to" and "to know how."

The third stage of parenting is parent as coach or manager of behavior. This stage essentially begins for us when our children reach adolescence. There is a great deal of overlap between this stage and the stage of parent as a guide and director. In early adolescence, children may require much more of a director, and they then will move into the stage of needing a coach. When we conceptualize parent as coach, it is helpful to think about the coach being on the sideline, always aware of what is happening in the game or on the field. The coach will allow the game to go forward as long as the game plan is being followed. The coach is the ultimate authority, and the players are aware of and accepting of this fact. Occasionally, a player may need to be put on the bench or be talked to about their performance. The same concept is easily generalized to parenting the adolescent.

During all stages of parenting, our goal is to teach and assist children in understanding that there are three family rules that are nonnegotiable. The family rules from the time children are very small are love, respect, and honesty. Love is unconditional acceptance of all family members, even when we disagree with one another. If family members become rejecting, shaming, or aggressive with one another, there is no longer unconditional acceptance or a loving relationship.

> The family rules from the time children are very small are *love*, *respect*, and *honesty*.

Respect is allowing other family members to have their own opinions and their own physical and emotional space. Violating boundaries is not respectful, nor is it loving. An example of boundary violation would be commenting, joking, or teasing about changes in a child or teen's body with another adult, or a family member going through a teen's room to take a look at his or her diary or journal. Disrespect can be a tone of voice, a disrespectful look, or simply ignoring in an attempt to show disrespect.

Honesty is telling one hundred percent of the truth one hundred percent of the time. I think it is helpful for children to see these family rules posted in the home on the refrigerator or in another central location. We build on these rules from a very young age, so by the time we get to the stage of parenting in which we are coach or manager, we can assist our adolescents in making healthy decisions based on those core rules. The family rules are actually core values that need to be integrated into each of our personalities so we all operate from a base of self-love, self-respect, and self-honesty.

Rick Gertsema

Using these three family rules also allows us to teach limits and boundaries throughout all of the stages of parenting. As difficult as it can be, we need to love our children enough to let them make mistakes, because we all learn through the courage of fixing our mistakes. By allowing our children to make mistakes, we can also model for them the three family values; out of love, respect, and honesty, we allow them to experience why a specific choice or decision is a poor one. A key point to understand is that even though they may have made a bad choice, made a bad decision, or shown a bad behavior, there is never such a thing as a bad kid. When children make mistakes, they quickly revert to feeling or saying, "I'm bad." They need help in differentiating between who they are as a person and the choices or behaviors they choose. We certainly want our children to feel remorse about a poor decision or a bad choice, which is what we commonly refer to as guilt. If children tell us they feel guilty about something they said or did, that is excellent. There is nothing negative about feeling guilty. However, if children start to believe that they are the mistake or they are the bad decision, we have entered into the arena of shame. *Not only did I make a bad decision, I am bad.* Shame is extremely unhealthy and causes major concerns in the areas of self-esteem, self-worth, and self-confidence.

Another golden rule, regardless of the stage of parenting, is never disagreeing in front of the children. Whichever parent has taken the lead in the discussion with the child, the other parent must follow that lead. Parents can disagree later, away from the children. Otherwise, a triangle will be created.

One of the things to keep in mind in all stages of parenting is that what is unresolved in your past will keep showing up until you get it fixed. There are many things that happened in our own childhoods and adolescence that can sometimes interfere with our healthy and desired patterns of parenting. There will be times during parenting that we will struggle with something that happened with us or to us. When we are involved in the most important role in our lives—being a parent—we will feel vulnerable and unsure of ourselves. This is typically because of something from our past. As an example, we may think that the child *acts just like I did when I was his age.* This will cause worries or fears for parenting. We may see ourselves acting just like our parents in terms of our parenting style when that is something we vowed never to do. As a general rule, if we are parenting out of fear or anger, it will not be effective parenting.

Keeping in mind the core family rules of love, respect, and honesty, it is important for parents to find a place to discuss things from the past that may interfere with family harmony. This can be done via individual or family therapy, family relationships, friendships, or parent support groups. There are also parenting classes available through local colleges and universities, county extension services, online, community education programming, and churches. Professionally, these services may also be found in local mental health clinics and mental health centers.

There are many fine books on parenting and development, as well as respectful, effective communication. There is a brief Suggested Resources section provided at the end of the book.

relationships

It is in the family that the soul takes seed.
—Thomas Moore

Let us put our minds together and see what kind of life we can make for our children.
—Sitting Bull

In order to foster healthy family relationships, family members must talk openly about the family rules. As previously discussed, love, respect, and honesty are core family values, and they need to be talked about at every opportunity. If relationships in the home are based on love, respect, and honesty, then children will learn to generalize those very same values in relationships outside of the home. Further, children and adolescents will also learn that they cannot give away what they don't have. In other words, in order to give love, respect, and honesty, they must have those values within. They must have a strong relationship with themselves in which they experience self-love, self-respect, and self-honesty.

Along these same lines in terms of love, respect, and honesty, it is important for children and adolescents to understand the concept of integrity. I like to remind children and adolescents that the word integrity starts with the letter *I*. This can also lead to some very good discussions about not being allowed to place the blame or responsibility on others—integrity starts with an *I*. An old saying that comes to mind with regard to integrity is, "You can talk the talk, but can you walk the walk?" This is an expression that older children and adolescents can readily understand.

Rick Gertsema

Often times, the relationship between a parent and child can get stuck. At those times, it can be very useful to do a hands-on exercise: The parent and the child sit facing each other. They hold up their hands, palms out, facing the other, and place the palms of their hands together. I encourage the parent and the child to push their hands toward each other with their open palms. This represents the relationship being stuck. I then explain that in healthy relationships there is always give and take. Sometimes a parent will take the lead; sometimes the child or adolescent will. I have them practice this with either the parent or the child beginning to move his or her hands and the other following that move. I then have them switch roles. It is very important that while doing this exercise, the parent and youth make direct eye contact with each other. This models a willingness to work together and openly communicate. Once the parent and the child understand this exercise, they can use it at home when there is a conflict or if it feels as though their relationship is stuck once again. It is important for parents and children to understand that it is very typical and normal for relationships to get stuck; the challenge is getting the relationship unstuck.

In terms of parenting, the relationship with your child needs to be clearly defined.

It is the children's job to push limits and look for structure. As the adult, it is imperative that you ensure that your child not be allowed to be the parent or the one in charge. Many times children need reassurance and consistent evidence that you will set limits and that you will maintain a healthy relationship with them based on love, respect, and honesty. They need to know that the parents are indeed in charge. Many times in adolescence, teens look to their parents and make statements about wanting their parent to be their friend. Adolescents need to be reminded that parents are much more than friends; they are people who will always be there for them through all of the stages of life. Friends may come and go, but parents are there unconditionally. This is the challenge of parenthood—to have the courage to work through your own past issues to the point where you can model being a fully-functioning adult to your children while offering them unconditional love and support through all the stages and phases of life. It is also very important to notice when children are doing something right and then tell them about it. One of

> Parents are much more than friends; they are people who will always be there for their children through all of the stages of life.

Rick Gertsema

the exercises that many parents find helpful is to put some kind of sticker on their watch or on the kitchen clock. It can be a smiley face or a similar sticker. As parents and adults, we are occupied with the time of day, and we often look at the clock or at our watches. The sticker serves as a reminder to find your child and catch them doing something right or doing something well. Far too many times, a parent-child relationship is based on requests, reminders, scolding, and prompting to get tasks completed, and we forget to praise our children when they are doing something well. Heartfelt appreciation expressed when children are simply being who they are—and doing so quietly—is a fine reinforcing strategy.

Many times, children and adolescents have a difficult time modulating or regulating their emotions. This can be very detrimental to the parent-child relationship. This will be covered more in-depth in the chapter on emotions management; however, a helpful analogy for parents and children is to know that it is okay to ride the emotional roller coaster. Children and adolescents often seem to ride a roller coaster of the ups and downs involved in their very emotional daily lives. The way to maintain a healthy relationship with your child is to stay on the ground, walk along, and watch your child while he or she rides. Once the child gets off the ride, based on relationship with parents, he or she may want to talk about what was happening that caused the ride on the roller coaster in the first place. Children and teenagers do not like parents to know or think that they are vulnerable.

Parenting strategies will be discussed in the chapter on discipline and routine. However, there is one strategy that is specific to the parent-child relationship. Parents can withdraw from the relationship with the child for very brief periods of time when the child or adolescent is having difficulty and is behaving disrespectfully or in an extremely emotional or agitated manner. It can be as clear as the following statement: "When you are ready to speak or act respectfully, I will make eye contact with you again."

Eye contact is a very important thing for all of us, especially for children and adolescents when they are having some difficulty. They look to our eyes for feedback, whether it is reassurance or other cues about what to do next. Typically, when using this intervention, eye contact is taken away for a couple of minutes, causing children to want to rejoin the relationship.

Sometimes, both children and adolescents will follow the parent around the house and demand that the parent *has* to talk to them. At those times, the parent can speak aloud in the third person and say

Rick Gertsema

something like, "I hear some noise, but I'm not sure what it is. If there is someone in the house who wants to talk to me, she would know that she needs to speak respectfully in order for me to respond right now." This serves as a reminder to the child or adolescent that there is a healthy way to rejoin the relationship.

It is also very important with small children, when using time-out procedures, to not make eye contact with the child on the way to a time-out. That could inadvertently negatively reinforce the behavior that is leading to the time-out.

Children love nothing more than having adults look directly into their eyes. When we are proud of our children or we really want to make a point, there is direct eye contact. When our children are sad or hurt, and we are trying hard to understand, we make direct eye contact. Not only can it give a strong sense of reassurance; it can also give the message that the adult is giving undivided attention. If a child has misbehaved, and the parent gives direct and intense eye contact all the way to time-out, the child could certainly act out again in order to get that kind of intense, uninterrupted focus and attention from the parent. The bottom line is that children crave our attention, whether good or bad. Withdraw attention, and behaviors tend to be extinguished. Give heartfelt, connected attention, and behaviors are reinforced— simple, yet sometimes hard to do.

communication

The first duty of love is to listen.

—Paul Tillich

If you've told a child a thousand times and he still doesn't understand, it is not the child who is a slow learner.

—Kari Fletcher

As mentioned, one of the key components to healthy communication is eye contact. When we think about eye contact, one thing to keep in mind is that the eyes are the window to the soul. There is no such thing as ugly eyes, no matter what the situation. This is especially critical at times of stress. As parents, when we are frustrated with our children, if we will look into our children's eyes, we will see their real emotion. It may be fear, worry, confusion, or frustration. When we don't look into our children's eyes, we are more likely to engage in power struggles. We tend to see the struggle as a "thing" rather than the inner turmoil of our child.

In a related arena are facial expressions. Many times, children and adolescents need help understanding what their facial expressions are communicating to others. It can be helpful for children to practice looking in a mirror. Parents can participate with their children as they are making specific faces. An additional outcome to this exercise is when parents recognize what their face may be communicating to their children. It can be shocking or at least surprising to adults when we see a look, such as a scowl, that has become habitual on our own face.

Although this may be a challenge, it is extremely important to observe and listen to what the behavior

Rick Gertsema

of a child is saying. Many times, children and adolescents cannot find words to express themselves. In fact, behavior does speak louder than words. If a child or teen's behavior is giving a parent the feeling that something is not right, then using open communication and the core family rules, children and adolescents can learn to express themselves using words.

For example, a child comes home from playing in the park and is acting out of sorts. A time when he should be more relaxed and settled because he has been at the park turns into restlessness. Out of love and concern, the parent may ask the child to go to his room for a few minutes to relax, and then the parent will come in to talk with them. It is not a consequence for the restlessness but more of a parental hunch that there is something not right. If the parent is honest with himself or herself, he will know there is something being said by the child's behavior.

The same can be true of a teenager who comes home from a Saturday night out, and her behavior is out of the ordinary. Turning a blind eye would be less than honest, so out of love, respect, and honesty, the parent talks to the teenager about what is happening. This demonstrates to teenagers that parents are being open, direct, and assertive with their concerns. It also can model healthy conflict resolution skills.

In addition to behavior, children and adolescents can communicate very effectively through drawings. Although drawing may be viewed as artwork or playing, it is often times a vehicle of expression and the child's language. When children or adolescents draw a picture, it is important that parents not ask, "What is this?" A more useful statement is, "Tell me about your picture." Children and adolescents are typically more than happy to talk about the picture. Parents can then point to very specific parts of the drawing or the picture and ask the child or adolescent to tell them about that specific thing. An expression of genuine interest with no judgment, criticism, or editing may lead to a greater understanding and connection between parent and child. Drawing, painting, or coloring can also be a calming activity for youth. These activities, done side-by-side with parents, can also enhance the parent-child relationship, even with older children.

During the school year, children and adolescents often have difficulty sharing things that may be bothering them from the school day. Here, we see the classic, "What happened at school today?" ques-

> When a child draws a picture, a more useful statement than, "What is this?" is, "Tell me about your picture."

Rick Gertsema

tion from the parent, followed by the hangdog response—"Nothing." It is helpful in these situations for children to know that during the day, they can write down their struggles or stressors on the back page of any notebook they have with them. Once they return home from school, they can review those notes with one or both parents. At that point in time, an open discussion about what happened during the school day can begin, and some problem-solving for use the next day may be able to happen.

Another tool that can be used to help youth communicate through writing is a communication notebook. This is a notebook that passes between parents and child, usually in a quiet and private manner. If a parent notices something positive or has a concern, the parent can write down this information and then set the notebook on the child's pillow. When the child is ready to read it, he will—at his convenience and in the safety of his room. The child can then respond to the entry in the notebook or write something totally unrelated. The notebook is then returned to the parents' room, and the parents can respond at their convenience. There is no verbal reminding about the notebook or any time limits on its use. It is simply another option to use for communication. All parties may come to discover that writing is an enjoyable and less stressful means of communicating about both the positive and challenging events of the day.

It is important to teach children and adolescents how to use "I" statements. When a sentence begins with the word "I," it can be very empowering and affirming. Remember—the word integrity starts with the letter *I*. It is even more empowering and affirming to *all* parties when we learn to make statements that start with "I feel" or "I believe." When it is established that there are no right or wrong beliefs or feelings, communication channels between children and parents become less loaded with emotion.

As children and adolescents grow, it can also be very helpful to pay close attention to the type of music to which they are listening. The theme of the music can be a good hint as to what is going on internally with the youth. Since most of us spend a great deal of time on the computer, it can be very effective to go online together and print off the lyrics to the music that they listen to on a regular basis. Those lyrics can then be read by the child and the parent. Again, this can lead to a very useful discussion about family values when done following the core family rules of love, honesty, and respect.

If children or adolescents are embarrassed or upset by this suggestion, it lets the parent know that

Rick Gertsema

the youth believes there is something inherently unhealthy about the music they are choosing. In a non-confrontational way, there can be a conversation opening with, "Help me understand why you listen to this music."

Also in the arena of communication, instant messaging has become a primary way for children and adolescents to communicate with one another. A very helpful rule is that if the screen is minimized by the youth when a parent walks by the computer, the computer will simply be turned off. There really is no reason for screens to be minimized unless the information on the screen is against the family rules. It is also good to have the computer in a central location in the home.

> A helpful rule is that if the screen is minimized by the youth when a parent walks by the computer, the computer will be turned off.

Another major form of communication with children and teenagers is text messaging. Parents need to trust the same sense of intuition with regard to the computer. If it feels like the child or adolescent is trying to hide something, it is time to explore that feeling. Parents do have the right as a responsible parent to read text messages and to use that as a teaching tool. Texting, like computer communication, gets out of hand quickly, and as parents we will need to monitor technology.

Often times, children and adolescents are allowed to have telephones, cell phones, computers, sound systems, and even television sets in their bedrooms. In addition, they may have their own VCRs and DVD players. Allowing all of this in the bedroom certainly is not conducive to practicing family values. It also does not lend itself to open and honest communication. The question that I will often pose to parents is whether they want to provide their child with an apartment in the family home; maybe not so tongue-in-cheek, I will comment that perhaps the youth should be paying rent for this lovely furnished apartment in his or her parents' home.

Taking a look at gender issues, we see that girls and boys definitely communicate differently. Boys typically operate with three basic premises: Know the rules, compete, and win. Another way to look at this is: Tell me what to do, tell me how to do it, and I will get it done. Boys are very linear in their thinking—they go from point A to point B with no stops in between.

Girls, on the other hand, most of the time operate through relationship. From the time girls are very

Rick Gertsema

young, they are involved in playing interactive games. They work through things by talking about and acting out their feelings; they are more apt to have sleepovers, and they typically have more relational-type birthday parties. The types of activities at a girl's party involve working together, playing games together for the experience of the interactions, and having a common task like decorating things. Girls are encouraged to work together in a non-competitive way to reach a consensus or result. Again, as a general rule, girls are able to multi-task, where boys can have difficulty in this regard. Boys are encouraged to compete and win.

However, what is common with both boys and girls is the concept of triangulation. The root word is triangle. Children and adolescents will try to get a third party involved so they are not directly accountable for their choices or behavior. If we envision the triangle, one side is the child, one side is the parent, and at the base of the triangle could be a friend, the other parent, a school situation, or a sibling. Triangulation is never healthy. Whenever a parent recognizes that there is a triangle being formed, their job is to flatten the triangle. Typically, triangulation will occur in a time of stress or challenge.

Major difficulties or crises in a child or adolescent's life are typically looked at as a negative thing. I try to teach parents and children that the Chinese character for crisis is literally made up of two words—danger and opportunity. By the time the specific crisis occurs, the danger has already transpired. The challenge is to find the opportunity within the crisis and use it to move forward from there.

Finally, during times of stress, apologies can be words that readily come out of a child or adolescent's mouth. "Sorry!" It can be very helpful for youth to understand that apologizing means two things; first, they feel bad, and second, they will try to change their behavior. A sense of integrity is achieved or acquired when we learn to ask for forgiveness. Further, "Sorry," without the word *I*, has no integrity.

Rick Gertsema

emotions
management

It is not attention the child is seeking but love.
—Sigmund Freud

Children learn through all their senses to develop a sense for order and logical thoughts.
—Maria Montessori

All children and adolescents need to be taught words to express their emotions. As we have seen, behavior, drawings, and music can be ways in which children and adolescents express their emotions. Ultimately, one of the greatest gifts we give children is the gift of words.

It can be very helpful for children and adolescents to learn to understand that anger is typically a secondary emotion. Anger is usually the lid that holds onto and holds in other emotions. The key is to discover what is beneath the anger. In the professional world, there is a common reference to children and adolescents needing to learn anger management; I prefer to think about emotions management. It is easy as human beings to say we are angry, but that really is not very descriptive. We can also use, "I was angry!" as an excuse or a way to try to get out of having an open discussion about the real issue or the real emotion.

I believe it is important for parents and children to understand that emotions are nothing more than a guide. They direct our response in certain situations. It is important to understand that there is no such thing as good emotions or bad emotions; all emotions are

> "I was angry!" is an excuse or a way to try to get out of having an open discussion about the real issue or emotion.

Rick Gertsema

simply a guide. There are, however, good behaviors and bad behaviors.

On the following pages, "feeling word vocabulary" sheets are provided for the three identified age groups. There are five primary categories of feelings that can be very helpful for children and adolescents to reference. A feeling word vocabulary sheet can be posted on a child's bulletin board or even on the refrigerator. It can assist the entire family in being able to identify emotions. I encourage parents to use the list and write down additional feeling words that are developmentally appropriate for their children. These become words that everyone can use on a regular basis to improve communication among family members.

Feeling Word Vocabulary

Infancy through age 6

HAPPY	SAD	ANGRY	SCARED	CONFUSED
Excited	Hurt	Furious	Afraid	Unsure
Terrific	Bad	Upset	Shocked	Surprised
Loved	Terrible	Mad	Shy	Uncomfortable
Cheerful	Upset	Frustrated	Nervous	Troubled

Feeling Word Vocabulary

Ages 7 through 12

HAPPY	SAD	ANGRY	SCARED	CONFUSED
Excited	Wounded	Furious	Fearful	Unsure
Terrific	Drained	Abused	Apprehensive	Trapped
Energized	Defeated	Hateful	Afraid	Surprised
Loved	Exhausted	Humiliated	Shocked	Distracted
Thrilled	Uncared for	Sabotaged	Startled	Uncomfortable
Marvelous	Rejected	Betrayed	Intimidated	Flustered
Valued	Terrible	Tense	Anxious	Undecided
Encouraged	Unwanted	Mad	Shy	Bothered
Joyful	Unloved	Used	Terrified	Troubled
Cheerful	Discarded	Frustrated	Nervous	Doubtful
Relieved	Upset	Controlled	Unsure	Awkward
Determined	Unappreciated	Irritated	Petrified	Puzzled
Confident	Discouraged	Exasperated	Doubtful	
Respected	Ashamed	Deceived	Insecure	
Admired	Distressed	Cheated	Defensive	
Relaxed	Lonely	Tricked	Uneasy	
Glad	Neglected		Threatened	
Good	Regretful			
Hopeful	Abandoned			
Pleased	Lost			
Flattered	Bad			

Rick Gertsema

Feeling Word Vocabulary

Ages 13 through 19

HAPPY	SAD	ANGRY	SCARED	CONFUSED
Excited	Devastated	Strangled	Fearful	Bewildered
Elated	Hopeless	Furious	Panicky	Trapped
Exuberant	Sorrowful	Seething	Afraid	Immobilized
Ecstatic	Depressed	Enraged	Shocked	Distracted
Terrific	Wounded	Hostile	Overwhelmed	Stagnant
Jubilant	Drained	Vengeful	Intimidated	Flustered
Energized	Defeated	Incensed	Desperate	Baffled
Enthusiastic	Exhausted	Abused	Frantic	Constricted
Loved	Helpless	Hateful	Terrified	Troubled
Thrilled	Crushed	Humiliated	Vulnerable	Ambivalent
Marvelous	Worthless	Sabotaged	Horrified	Awkward
Justified	Uncared for	Betrayed	Petrified	Puzzled
Resolved	Dejected	Repulsed	Appalled	Disorganized
Valued	Rejected	Rebellious	Full of dread	Foggy
Gratified	Humbled	Outraged	Tormented	Perplexed
Encouraged	Empty	Tense	Hesitant	
Optimistic	Miserable	Fuming	Threatened	
Joyful	Distraught	Exploited	Uneasy	
Proud	Deserted	Throttled	Defensive	
Cheerful	Grievous	Mad	Insecure	
Relieved	Burdened	Spiteful	Skeptical	
Assured	Demoralized	Patronized	Apprehensive	
Determined	Condemned	Vindictive	Suspicious	
Grateful	Terrible	Used	Alarmed	
Appreciative	Unwanted	Repulsed	Shaken	
Confident	Unloved	Ridiculed	Swamped	

Chart 3 continued

HAPPY	SAD	ANGRY	SCARED	CONFUSED
Respected	Mournful	Resentful	Startled	Misunderstood
Admired	Pitiful	Disgusted	Guarded	Doubtful
Delighted	Discarded	Smothered	Stunned	Bothered
Alive	Disgraced	Frustrated	Awed	Undecided
Fulfilled	Disheartened	Stifled	Reluctant	Uncomfortable
Tranquil	Despised	Offended	Anxious	Uncertain
Relaxed	Upset	Controlled	Shy	Surprised
Glad	Inadequate	Peeved	Nervous	Unsettled
Good	Dismal	Annoyed	Unsure	Unsure
Satisfied	Unappreciated	Agitated	Timid	
Peaceful	Discouraged	Irritated	Concerned	
Hopeful	Ashamed	Exasperated	Perplexed	
Fortunate	Distressed	Harassed	Doubtful	
Pleased	Distant	Anguished	Timid	
Flattered	Disillusioned	Deceived		
	Lonely	Aggravated		
	Neglected	Perturbed		
	Isolated	Provoked		
	Alienated	Dominated		
	Regretful	Coerced		
	Apathetic	Cheated		
	Resigned	Uptight		
	Drained	Dismayed		
	Bad	Tolerant		
	Degraded	Displeased		
	Lost			
	Disturbed			
	Wasted			
	Abandoned			

Rick Gertsema

The vocabulary sheet can be used in situations from a very young age through the last developmental stage of adolescence at the age of nineteen. One of the key concepts to teach children and adolescents is that nobody can make another person feel anything. Our response and our reaction are totally under our control. Nobody can make you angry, and nobody can make you sad. "I am in charge of my emotions." Note the importance of using "I" statements. The goal is to teach children and adolescents that none of us really wants other people to be in charge of our emotions or our responses.

For all age groups, the children or adolescents can identify one of the five emotions at the top of the page to begin their discussion of what they are feeling. They can also pick one of the many words under the five categories and talk about the primary feeling. Parents can also pick words that they think accurately describe what they are observing. Again, all of this lends itself to good discussion and problem-solving.

Many times, children and adolescents get stuck emotionally and don't want to or are unable to talk about what they are feeling. If there is a good emotional foundation and a strong relationship, sometimes one of the best ways to get a child to open up is to help them talk openly about their anger. Once a child or adolescent is talking about their anger, they may become more spontaneous and use some of the words they have learned to describe where they are. They can even use the vocabulary sheet and point to words rather than verbalizing them.

The key with emotion management is to teach children and adolescents that they are always in charge of their emotions and what they choose to do with those emotions. This is a concept that can cause great difficulty for children and adults. Much of what we see depicted on television, in movies, in books and comic books, and in video games falsely indicates that humans cannot help but *react* to others rather than *respond* from within themselves.

If a child or adolescent is struggling with a clinical issue such as depression, anxiety, attention deficit hyperactivity disorder, or other disorders, the parents are then responsible to help the child or adolescent to learn he or she is still responsible to be proactive in the management of their concerns. This may entail going to therapy, counseling and/or responsibly complying with taking medications. We do not want to teach "pick yourself up by the bootstraps" mentality, rather a mentality of "we are all responsible for our choices, and we need to deal with those choices in a responsible manner." It is not about fault or blame; it is about responsibility.

Rick Gertsema

discipline
/routine

It is a gift to a child to have a home where there is authority. When kids can predict what's coming, they can learn to self-regulate.

—Connie Abbott

We adults are the ones who define bad behavior without showing alternative behaviors. This is the big difference between discipline and punishment. Discipline teaches what to do.

—Vicki Thrasher Cronin

87

In the arenas of discipline and routine, there are several very important concepts. The first is that it is always better to be proactive than reactive. Although this sounds fairly simple, once emotions are running high, it is not so easily accomplished. It takes much more energy to put out fires and run from one fire to another than it does to have a straightforward, comprehensive escape plan. It is not a question of *whether* there will be conflict or the need for discipline/routine with children and adolescents. It is simply a matter of *when* we will need some type of intervention. Hence, the more parents are in a proactive frame of mind, the better.

The second concept with regard to discipline and routine is that there is absolutely no substitute for consistency. Being able to be consistent as a parenting team is optimal. If there has been a divorce or separation in the family, consistency within each home is most important. Many parents believe that there must be consistency between the homes. However, that is not absolutely necessary. Children and adolescents will learn discipline and routine that is specific to each family's home.

There are two times during the day that routine is especially important. The morning routine, especially during the school year, is important. As much as possible, everything needs to be planned ahead of time

Rick Gertsema

and be predictable. The optimal morning routine is to wake up to an alarm. Once the alarm goes off, the parent can use one verbal prompt to start the morning routine. Some children and adolescents prefer to shower in the morning, others at night. Bathroom routine is established, getting dressed is typically next, and finally, there is some kind of breakfast before the day begins. Of course, there will be variations, and there will need to be some coordination with households where there is more than one child. However, these times can be made into a routine that is very predictable for all of the children. A smooth start to the day makes everyone's life easier.

The second time of day that routine is important is bedtime. At this time of day, children and adolescents need to have quiet time in order for them to fall asleep. It is also beneficial for them to have time to be alone. This usually involves crawling into bed and reading or doing a similar activity. Then, there is a designated time for lights out. As children grow, it is a great feeling of accomplishment when they are able to turn off their own lights without any prompting.

During the quiet time before sleep, parents can also build in a routine of talk time; this is simply giving the child or adolescent ten minutes of the parents sitting in the bedroom. If the youth wants to talk, that is great. If they choose not to talk, simply stay in their room and do another activity. It is a wonderful message to give a child or adolescent that there are ten minutes at the end of the day that are devoted just to them.

> During the quiet time before sleep, parents can also build in a routine of talk time, regardless of the stage of development.

For summertime and for preschool children, it can also be helpful to have a mid-afternoon quiet time. This can be a very intentional time for parents and children to go to their rooms and have time for themselves. For younger children, this may be a time when they fall asleep if they really are tired. It can be a bridge from nap time to the time in which children don't need a nap. It can also give parents a predictable quiet time in which they can complete some of their tasks.

During the school year, it can also be helpful to have this mid-afternoon quiet time. When children come home, and everyone is reunified after a hectic day at school, the level of chaos in the home can rise significantly. For that reason, it may be helpful to have everyone go to their rooms to unpack their backpacks, retrieve any papers of which parents need to be aware, and then come to the kitchen for a snack. This mid-

Rick Gertsema

afternoon quiet time could be as short as ten or fifteen minutes. Children and adolescents may find that they like more than just fifteen minutes.

Finally, although it can be very difficult, having one meal together each day is a wonderful routine to establish and maintain. Certainly, with busy schedules, it may not be easy to accommodate. Families may not always be able to eat at home. However, there are very creative ways, even with fast food, that families can still enjoy one meal a day together.

In regard to discipline, it is important to differentiate between discipline and punishment. I try to help families understand that the root word of discipline is disciple, and disciple means *to teach*. When we discipline our children, we are trying to teach different behaviors and healthy choices. We do not need to focus on the negative behavior or the unhealthy choices, just how to move forward in a different, and hopefully better, way. Children and adolescents have a great deal of energy, and sometimes they are waiting for somebody to step in front of the train, so to speak—to slow things down for them. In many situations, children and adolescents are not confident that they have the necessary skills to slow things down on their own. Saying no can be one of the most reassuring things in the entire world. Of course, on the outside, a child or adolescent would not let on that he or she was actually looking for that answer.

On to consequences! It is not the size of a consequence but the certainty and predictability that the consequence will be delivered that counts. Many times, out of frustration, things will come out of a parent's mouth that he or she really has no intention of implementing. Examples may include taking away a bicycle for two weeks, no television for two weeks, grounding the child in the house for one month, or no use of the telephone or the computer for one month.

As much as possible, consequences need to be delivered in such a way that every day can be a new beginning. In other words, a consequence will hopefully not last longer than one day. One day is an eternity for a child or adolescent. If he or she feels like the consequence will go on for several days, waking up in the morning will be even less of an enjoyable experience. This will set the stage for the next several days, and children will feel like they are starting the day in a "one down" position. None of us, including parents, want to start the day in a one down position. Furthermore, they will have nothing to gain or lose by more acting out behavior, as they are already

Rick Gertsema

grounded or experiencing the ongoing consequence. Consequences beyond a couple of days are not likely helpful to anyone. Grounding for a week will be a punishment for the entire family and teaching will likely not happen. Instead, it will be an exercise in power and/or control of the child or adolescent. Of course, there will be difficult behaviors that occur in the evening hours, and the child or adolescent will then need to complete their consequence the next day. Keep in mind that we are delivering consequences in order to teach our youth. We are not trying to punish ourselves. This is often what happens when a child is suspended from school. The child gets to stay home, and the parent is left experiencing the consequence.

When we think about consequences and discipline, we once again go back to the core family rules of love, respect, and honesty. If you get a clenched jaw, it is important to be honest with yourself and realize that you may need to stop talking right now, or you may need to lower your voice. If a power struggle with a child or adolescent is in progress, create a respectful and honest non-verbal cue that one parent can use to help the other out of the struggle. This can be a friendly hand on the shoulder or making a hand signal to indicate a need for time-out.

Finally, it is okay for parents to give themselves a time-out and come back when they are regulated and ready. This is an excellent opportunity for modeling behavior to children and adolescents. It shows them that the youth is not in charge of the parents' behavior or the parents' reaction. It also demonstrates that a time-out can be helpful for all of us.

Along these same lines, if you are feeling stuck as a parent, you can ask your adolescent, "What do you expect me to do in response to this situation? If you cannot come up with something, I certainly will." Many times, adolescents will come up with very severe consequences—much more severe than parents would impose. Asking your adolescent this question also allows parents some extra time to come up with reasonable consequences.

Part of discipline is setting expectations for children. It seems most helpful when parents set the expectation, either verbally or in writing, and then give their child or adolescent choice A or choice B to meet that specific expectation. The bottom line is that the parents set the expectation, the child will meet that expectation, and the world will stop until the expectation is met. That may mean that the child or adolescent may not watch television, be on the computer, or engage in other activities. If a parent can't come up with choices immediately, he or she can simply take time to think and then come back in a couple of minutes. A clear example is that a child's bedroom will be totally cleaned every Saturday by noon. This is the expectation. The child can either do it by himself, or at noon a parent or both parents will come in with a garbage bag to help. If the parent comes in, whatever they pick up is put in the garbage bag, and the parent will dispose of the contents of the bag. This is choice A or choice B.

The same principle applies to setting expectations before going out in public to places like the mall or the grocery store. Let children and adolescents know the expectations and what will happen if the expectations are not met. When this is first being implemented, it may be helpful if both parents are along or a friend is along to help with follow-through.

A consequence list may be posted on the refrigerator. Consequences can be typical daily chores that are performed by every member of the family: a random act of kindness or a positive interaction that needs to be completed with siblings or parents. If family rules have been broken, the behavior can be rated as a minor, moderate, or major infraction of family rules. As an example, if one family rule is broken, one consequence or chore needs to be chosen and completed.

If it is a moderate offense, two chores need to be completed, and if it is a major offense, three chores would have to be completed. Again, the world will stop until the consequences or chores are completed. The child or adolescent will need to come to the parent stating that he or she has completed the chosen consequences for things to move forward. It is the youth's responsibility to initial the chart and verify that the needed chore has been completed. The chores need to be completed one vertical column at a time; otherwise, a child will pick the same chore time after time.

On occasion, children and adolescents will make such statements as, "You can't make me," in terms of complying with the consequence list. This is a true statement, but the youth needs to be reminded that if there is not compliance, that is disrespectful and is against one of the family rules. Children can be told that if they cannot be respectful to parents, their world will stop until they demonstrate that they can show respect within the home. They will also need to complete the chore from the consequence list, or they will have grounded themselves.

If there has been a history of difficulties within and/or outside the home, many parents find it of utmost importance that children and adolescents be honest in order to earn back trust. In keeping with the

Rick Gertsema

family rules of love, respect, and honesty, many parents will consider that if a child or adolescent is being 100 percent honest, there may not be a consequence. If there is a consequence, it is typically mild.

As discussed in a previous chapter, because of emotional highs and lows, it may appear as though children and adolescents are riding on a roller coaster. Consider that children's and adolescents' job is to carry around a rope for a power struggle or an emotional tug-of-war. When we keep in mind that children constantly throw us that rope, we remember that *our* job is to not pick it up. It can be very affirming for parents to make this statement out loud: "I am not picking up the rope!"

Don't pick up the rope! This is not tug-of-war.

Another of the most frustrating challenges in parenting is sibling discord, whether it is fighting, tattling, or other disrespectful interactions. If two or more children are fighting, and you don't know who started it, everybody gets a time-out. This is a concept known as a shutdown. Shutdowns can be implemented at any time the parents believe it would be beneficial for everyone to go to his or her room or to another neutral area to diffuse the energy within the home. When parents feel that they are in some type of investigative position, trying to figure out who started what, it is a great time for a shutdown.

Rick Gertsema

summary

It is my sincere hope that what you have read in these pages will prove to be helpful to you and your family. It is a compilation of many hours, months, and years of experience spending time with children, adolescents, parents, and families. I truly believe that with love, respect, and honesty, all things are possible—even peaceful parenting.

Our children did not come to us with an instruction manual. That would have been a useful thing! What they bring to us are experiences and avenues for growth in compassion and understanding. As we parent our children and nurture their growth and development, we make the world a better place.

May we keep in mind that all of our interactions with children—even the most stressful ones—are blessings when we allow love, respect, and honesty to be our guides.

Rick Gertsema

suggested
resources

How to Talk so Kids Listen by Adele Faber, Elaine Mazlish, and Kimberly Ann Coe (Illustrator)

Siblings Without Rivalry: How to Help Your Children Live Together So You Can Live Too by Adele Faber and Elaine Mazlish

Ending the Homework Hassle by John Rosemond

John Rosemond's Six–Point Plan: for Raising Happy, Healthy Children by John Rosemond

Making the "Terrible" Two's Terrific by John Rosemond

Teen-Proofing: Fostering Responsible Decision Making in Your Teenager by John Rosemond

How to Hug a Porcupine: Negotiating the Prickly Points of the Teen Years by Julie Ross

The Blessing of a Skinned Knee by Wendy Mogel

No: Why Kids-of all ages-Need to Hear It and Why Parents Can Say It by David Walsh

Why Do They Act That Way?: A Survival Guide to the Adolescent Brain for You and Your Teen by David Walsh.

Rick Gertsema